# Dancing Bey(
# Inspirational Journey of Chris
# McCausland on Strictly Come Dancing

*How a Blind Comedian Redefined Resilience, Representation, and Determination Through Dance.*

## LANCE R. KOUBA

© 2025 [LANCE R. KOUBA]. All rights reserved. No part of this book may be reproduced, distributed, or transmitted in any form or by any means, including photocopying, recording, or other electronic or mechanical methods, without the prior written permission of the publisher, except in the case of brief quotations embodied in critical reviews and certain other noncommercial uses permitted by copyright law.

# TABLE OF CONTENTS

Introduction: Stepping Into the Spotlight................... 6

Chapter 1: A Life Transformed........................9

    Chris's early years and diagnosis with retinitis pigmentosa................10

    The challenges of losing his sight and how he navigated a changing world................... 12

    Introduction to Chris's career in comedy and how humor became his tool for resilience.....................14

Chapter 2: The Call to Dance........................ 17

    The invitation to join *Strictly Come Dancing* and Chris's initial reaction...................19

    The decision to step into a completely new world of dance, against the backdrop of public expectations............ 21

Chapter 3: Meeting Dianne: Trust and Teamwork.. 25

    Chris's partnership with professional dancer Dianne Buswell.......................27

    How they built a strong bond of trust and communication from the start............................. 30

    The unique methods they used to teach choreography without sight................................. 31

Chapter 4: Dancing Without Boundaries.................. 35

    Behind-the-scenes training and the challenges of learning intricate routines........................36

    The role of tactile cues, verbal guidance, and emotional connection in mastering the dances....37

    How Chris adapted to the intense scrutiny of the

judges and live audiences.......................................... 41

Chapter 5: The Dance Floor: A New Arena............... 45

    Highlights from Chris's first few performances. 46

    The emotional rollercoaster of rehearsals, mistakes, and triumphs............................................ 48

    Fan reactions, audience support, and growing public affection for Chris........................................ 51

Chapter 6: The Glitterball Dream............................. 55

    The pivotal moments in the competition that defined Chris's journey............................................ 56

    Key performances that earned high praise from the judges and fans.................................................. 58

    The significance of each routine beyond the technical execution.................................................. 61

Chapter 7: Breaking Barriers, Changing Perceptions. 64

    How Chris's success on *Strictly Come Dancing* challenged societal norms about disability and ability...................................................................... 65

    The impact of his journey on the broader conversation around representation in entertainment......................................................... 69

Chapter 8: Triumph and Heartache: The Emotional Journey..................................................................... 73

    The highs and lows of Chris's time on *Strictly Come Dancing*....................................................... 74

    Personal moments of doubt, growth, and discovery................................................................. 76

    The profound emotional impact of his journey on

Chris and those around him.................................. 79

Chapter 9: The Final Dance: Victory Beyond the Glitterball.................................................................. 82

The moment Chris and Dianne won the Glitterball Trophy.................................................. 83

Reflections on what the victory meant to Chris and the disability community................................. 87

How the win became a symbol of determination, resilience, and the power of inclusivity................ 89

Chapter 10: Legacy of a Champion............................ 91

Chris's life after *Strictly Come Dancing*: how the experience reshaped his career and public image............................................................................ 92

The lasting influence of his journey on the entertainment industry and viewers alike........... 95

How Chris continues to advocate for inclusivity, visibility, and empowerment.................................. 96

CONCLUSION............................................................ 98

A reflection on Chris's journey and the ongoing message of hope and perseverance...................... 99

Final thoughts on the broader impact of his story and how it continues to inspire people worldwide.. 100

## Introduction: Stepping Into the Spotlight

Under the bright glare of stage lights, Chris McCausland had long been a master of his profession. Armed with a keen wit and a distinct viewpoint, he'd developed a career that had audiences doubling over in laughter. Yet, even in his most inventive times, he might not have seen himself exchanging punchlines for pirouettes. The world of ballroom dancing, with its complicated choreography and relentless physical demands, appeared a totally separate realm. But when the chance came knocking, Chris didn't simply answer—he grabbed it with wide arms.

Chris's path to Strictly Come Dancing wasn't an escape from his comic beginnings but a development of his narrative. Comedy had taught him the art of timing, the confidence to go into the unknown, and the power of connecting with an audience. Dancing, as he quickly realized, would push those same talents in ways he had never expected. The choice to join the famous television show was not only about learning to dance but also rethinking what was possible.

From the minute Chris confirmed his involvement, whispers of interest swelled into waves of enthusiasm. How would a man who has never seen the dazzle of a sequin overcome the demands of a competition noted for its high-pressure routines and rigorous attention to detail? Chris, meanwhile, had no interest in playing to doubts or limits. For him, the challenge was in understanding how far trust, tenacity, and creativity could go him.

The relationship with Dianne Buswell, a seasoned dancer with a reputation for breaking molds, marked the beginning of an exceptional cooperation. Together, they would explore unknown ground, utilizing tactile direction, verbal signals, and unwavering confidence in one another to perfect routines that defied expectations.

Stepping into this new environment was no minor accomplishment. The tournament was a maelstrom of physical strain, emotional intensity, and public scrutiny. But Chris wasn't one to shy away from a challenge. Each moment on the dance floor was an opportunity—not simply to move but to tell a narrative, to connect, and to illustrate that the boundaries we see are frequently those we establish for ourselves.

Strictly Come Dancing is a stage where artists strive for excellence with every step. For Chris, though, the journey was never about flawless execution. It was about embracing vulnerability and pushing boundaries, both his own and those imposed by others. As he prepared for his first performance, the spotlight shifted, not just onto his story, but onto the countless others who would find hope and inspiration in his every move.

## Chapter 1: A Life Transformed

Chris McCausland's first recollections were painted in brilliant hues. He could recall the vivid blue of his favorite toy car, the golden rays that flowed through the living room windows on peaceful Sunday mornings, and the way his mother's garden appeared alive with bursts of red and yellow. The landscape he grew up in was not merely seen but felt—alive with the type of implicit potential that comes with a young boy's unfettered amazement. But as he developed, things began to alter. It started gently, almost imperceptibly, like a darkness sneaking into the borders of his vision.

Chris was nine when he first recognized things wasn't quite right. Playing football with pals in the park, he found himself stumbling over the ball, missing passes he claimed he'd seen coming. At first, he shrugged it off, chalking it up to carelessness or preoccupation. But with time, the events became increasingly common.

His parents noticed too—the way he peered at the television, the hesitancy in his movements, the occasional slip on familiar pathways.

A visit to the optician eventually led into a referral to a specialist. Chris, still too little to realize the weight of what was occurring, held his father's hand tightly as they sat in the clean white room. The doctor's words, stated with professional clarity, sliced through the air: retinitis pigmentosa. The phrase meant little to Chris then, but the gloomy tone in his parents' voices as they asked question after inquiry told him plenty. This was serious.

*Chris's early years and diagnosis with retinitis pigmentosa.*

Retinitis pigmentosa was explained to Chris in simple terms: a gradual disorder affecting the retina, steadily decreasing the field of vision until it was gone. For a youngster who loved the outdoors, who enjoyed the freedom of roaming across wide fields and the simple delight of watching cartoons, the diagnosis seemed like an unseen thief had entered his life. But at that time, Chris wasn't thinking about the future. He was thinking about the now—the confusing, heavy stillness in the car ride home, the unsaid anxiety in his mother's wrinkled forehead as she cooked supper that evening.

Over the years, the illness worsened precisely as the physicians expected. By his adolescent years, the world around him began to blur, colors melting into muted tones, edges of objects dissolving into shadows. Friends at school were sympathetic, but even their well-meaning actions sometimes seemed like a reminder of what he was losing. Teachers, unsure how to adjust, sometimes talked in quiet tones that communicated sorrow. For Chris, the worst aspect wasn't the gradual loss of sight—it was the loss of routine.

Yet, even at those moments of frustration and grief, there was something in Chris that refused to give in. He adapted. When the football games grew too risky, he took refuge in listening to matches on the radio, visualizing the moves in his mind with vivid clarity. When reading became a problem, he resorted to audiobooks, finding himself in stories that carried him far from the restrictions of his life. Chris was learning, even then, to navigate a world that was no longer played by the old rules.

*The challenges of losing his sight and how he navigated a changing world.*

By the time Chris reached his twenties, his vision had all but vanished. The darkness that once felt like a looming menace had become a frequent friend. But Chris, ever the pragmatic, refused to let it define him. He treated his blindness not as a barrier but as a challenge—a problem to solve, a new way to perceive the world.

It was during this period that Chris learned the power of comedy. He found that people were often uncomfortable talking about his blindness, tiptoeing around the issue or ignoring it completely. So, he resolved to address it head-on. At family gatherings, he began cracking jokes about his disability, converting awkward silences into bursts of laughing. Humor, he learned, wasn't simply a method to put others at ease—it was a way to retake power.

The first time Chris stepped onto a stage, it wasn't planned. He was at an open mic night, pulled there by pals who demanded he give it a go. Nervously grasping the microphone, he began recalling the absurdities of navigating life without sight—the time he unintentionally tried to get into the wrong car, the way people yelled at him as if blindness also meant deafness. The room exploded in laughter. For Chris, it was a revelation.

Comedy wasn't only a method to communicate his experiences; it was a way to connect. On stage, he wasn't "the blind guy" or a symbol of pity. He was Chris McCausland, a storyteller who could make people laugh, ponder, and view the world from his perspective.

*Introduction to Chris's career in comedy and how humor became his tool for resilience.*

As the years went by, Chris polished his art. His early engagements were small—pubs, bars, the occasional community event—but each performance boosted his confidence. Audiences reacted to his sincerity, his ability to find humor in circumstances that others may shy away from. He laughed about the peculiarities of accessibility, the bizarre experiences with strangers who sought to "help," and the way people frequently believed blindness equaled an inability to live a full life.

Chris's comedy wasn't simply funny—it was smart, relevant, and very human. He didn't shy away from the heavy material, but he conveyed it with a lightness that made people laugh even as they reflected. His routines weren't only about blindness; they were about life, resilience, and the absurdity of the human experience.

Before quickly, Chris found himself on grander stages. Television appearances followed, along with a growing audience that loved not just his comedy but his philosophy. Chris had transformed what many perceived as a hindrance into his greatest strength. He wasn't just a comedian—he was a voice for anybody who had ever felt misjudged or misunderstood.

**A LIFE TRANSFORMED**

Looking back, Chris frequently thought on the road that took him to this place. The youngster who once dreaded the gathering darkness has discovered a way to flourish inside it. His blindness, although unquestionably tough, had turned him into the guy he was—a man who could find joy in the darkest circumstances, who could stand on a platform and make strangers feel connected.

For Chris, the transition wasn't simply about adapting to blindness. It was about learning who he was outside it. Comedy provided him a platform, but it was his resilience, his capacity to face life's uncertainties, that truly characterized him. And as he prepared to walk into the world of ballroom dancing, he took with him the lessons learnt from a lifetime of challenges: that humor is a strong weapon, that connection is vital, and that even in the face of hardship, there is always light to be discovered.

## Chapter 2: The Call to Dance

The late afternoon sunshine crept through the blinds of Chris McCausland's living room, forming faint patterns on the carpet. He sat on the edge of his old leather sofa, the faint perfume of his half-drunk cup of tea floating nearby. The day had been uneventful until the phone arrived. His phone vibrated, skittering slightly across the coffee table. Picking it up, he recognized the number—a producer from the BBC.

"What could they possibly want now?" he whispered under his breath, more amused than annoyed. He had done a few panel programs for them in the past, shared a few chuckles about his comic routines, but this felt out of the blue. Sliding his thumb across the screen, he responded with his customary cheery tone. "Alright, who's looking for a laugh today?"

The voice on the other end sounded measured yet eager. They didn't waste time. "Chris, we have an idea, and we think you'd be perfect for it."

Chris sat back against the sofa, hesitant yet fascinated. "Go on, then," he said, already attempting to predict the joke.

"Strictly Come Dancing. We'd like you to be part of the next season."

For a minute, the words didn't land. He stopped, uncertain if this was a joke or some elaborate misunderstanding. "Strictly?" he repeated, his voice raising incredulously. "You do realize I can't see, don't you? Or has that piece evaded you?"

The producer giggled quietly but stayed strong. "We know, Chris. That's part of why we think you'd be incredible. It's not just about dancing—it's about narrative, connecting, showing people what's possible."

Chris squirmed uneasily, the phone pressed closely against his ear. The prospect of walking into a world of glitz, glamor, and pirouettes was ludicrous. He'd mastered the art of standing still with a microphone, making people laugh with words and timing. But dancing? That wasn't just outside his comfort zone; it felt like stepping into another dimension.

"Let me think about it," he finally said, his tone cautious but not dismissive.

*The invitation to join \*Strictly Come Dancing\* and Chris's initial reaction.*

The following several days were a frenzy of ideas, doubts, and many interactions with family and friends. His wife, Patricia, was the first to weigh in. "It's mad," she murmured, her voice filled with a combination of wonder and encouragement as they sat together at the kitchen table. "But you've never backed down from mad before."

Chris rubbed the bridge of his nose, the weight of the decision pressing down. "It's not just mad, though, is it? This isn't a gig I can bluff my way through with a joke. This is physical, live, in front of millions. People will expect... something. And what if I can't deliver?"

Patricia reached across the table, her hand finding his. "You've spent your whole life proving people wrong. This is no different."

Still, the doubts lingered. He thought about the viewers, the scrutiny, the inevitable whispers about whether someone like him could even attempt such a feat. Chris had never shied away from being the blind guy on stage—it was part of his identity, his humor—but this felt like inviting the entire nation into his vulnerability.

The producer called again, their enthusiasm unwavering. They spoke of the possibilities, the opportunity to inspire, the chance to show people a side of him they hadn't seen before.

"This isn't just about dancing, Chris. It's about rethinking what's possible."

It was that phrase—"redefining what's possible"—that resonated with him. Late at night, as he lay awake in bed, he thought about his daughter. What kind of example would he be setting if he let fear dictate his decisions? She didn't view him as restricted, just as Dad, the man who could make her grin with a goofy voice or help her negotiate the world with her own kind of courage.

By the time he made his choice, it wasn't with a sense of surety but with a calm resolve. "Alright," he told the producer on their next call. "Let's give it a go."

> The decision to step into a completely new world of dance, against the backdrop of public expectations.

As word circulated about his involvement, the media hummed with speculation. Headlines ranged from sympathetic to dubious, with some asking whether it was fair to have a blind participant in such a difficult event. Chris attempted to ignore the sounds, but it was hard to escape fully. He could feel the weight of public expectation bearing down on him like an unseen hand.

Friends called to wish him success, their voices tinted with a combination of respect and doubt. "You're braver than me, mate," one remarked. Another commented, "I don't know how you're going to do it, but if anyone can, it's you."

The first day of filming seemed weird. The cameras whirred quietly as he and Dianne stood together in front of the classic Strictly backdrop. The glittering outfits of other candidates shimmered slightly in the distance, their intensity evident even to Chris, who couldn't see their delight. He could hear the rustle of cloth, the clicking of heels on the floor, and the mumble of producers giving last-minute orders.

"Ready?" Dianne questioned, her fingertips barely stroking his arm.

"Not even close," he said, a nervous grin growing across his face. But he took a deep breath and went forward, feeling the full intensity of the spotlight—not only the physical one but the figurative glare of millions of eyes watching, eager to see what he would do.

## A LEAP OF FAITH

In those early days, Chris's confidence faltered often. The exercises felt impossibly difficult, the steps a tangled web of movements that his body refused to understand. He tripped, lost his balance, and murmured self-deprecating comments to mask his irritation. But Dianne was unrelenting in her encouragement, breaking down each action into digestible portions, using her voice and touch to lead him through.

"Don't think about the end result," she would advise. "Just focus on the next step."

And slowly, step by step, things began to move. Chris found himself not only studying but feeling the beat of the music, the flow of the moves. He stopped thinking about how he looked and started trusting his instincts, his partner, and the process.

## Chapter 3: Meeting Dianne: Trust and Teamwork

The rehearsal studio door creaked open, pouring the muted murmur of hurrying producers and the faint rhythm of a pop song from the room next door into the silent corridor. Chris McCausland hesitated, adjusting his grasp on the white cane he habitually held securely in his palm, though he seldom used it indoors. The air inside was chilly, almost frigid, with the slight scent of varnished wood and a trace of lemon from the recently polished floors. He could hear the expanse of the room around him—the echo of faraway footsteps, the slight whoosh of air when the door slammed shut behind him.

He felt the slight weight of expectancy pushing against him, a familiar sense that preceded every new performance location. But this wasn't a stage, and he wasn't here to do stand-up. This was something altogether new, and it left him unexpectedly off-balance.

"Chris!" a cheery, enthusiastic voice cried from across the room, piercing through his meandering thoughts. The Australian accent instantly struck a warm, inviting tone. The steps that followed were light and fast, each one getting louder as they neared.

"I'm Dianne," she replied brightly, offering a hand before thinking he might not instantly notice. With a brief giggle, she adjusted, delicately stroking his shoulder instead. "Sorry! I'm grasping your hand now—there we go. Official handshake accomplished."

Chris couldn't help but grin at her effortless assurance. Her grip was hard yet cordial, her palms roughened by years of dancing training. "Good to meet you, Dianne," he added, his voice conveying an edge of his customary self-deprecating humor. "Just a heads-up—I'm really good at standing still. The rest... well, let's just say the jury's still out."

"Oh, you're going to be fantastic," she exclaimed without hesitation, her tone filled with enthusiasm. "And standing still? Perfect start. We'll grow from there."

> Chris's partnership with professional dancer Dianne Buswell.

Their first session together wasn't about dance. It was about orientation—both of the room and each other. Dianne took the lead, describing the chamber with a degree of detail that was almost dramatic. "We've got mirrors along the entire front wall," she added, approaching him closer and guiding his palm to touch the chilly, reflected surface. "Not super useful for you, I know, but they're there. On the far left is the barre—great for warming up or hanging onto when we're trying something hard. The floor's solid wood, no odd dips or fissures, I promise."

Her voice was calm, her words clear without being overbearing. She took him across the area slowly, letting him feel the arrangement of furniture and props, the wide width of the dance floor, and even the positioning of their water bottles on a little table in the corner.

"Here's the deal," she continued as they returned to the center of the room. "You don't have to remember everything right away. That's my job. We're a team now. My eyes, your steps—we've got this."

The confidence in her statements was infectious. Chris nodded, already feeling the first tendrils of trust building. "Alright," he answered, smiling weakly. "Let's see if I can manage not to trip over my own feet."

**LEARNING THE LANGUAGE OF DANCE**
The first exercise was deceptively simple: walking in sync to music. Dianne stood next to Chris, laying his hand on her shoulder. "Okay," she responded, her tone level. "We're going to

walk together. Small steps, nothing spectacular. I'll count us in."

The music began—a slow, steady pace that pulsed through the studio like a metronome. Dianne counted loudly, her voice calm and steady. "One, two, three, four. Now step with me."

Chris moved gingerly at first, his movements slightly out of pace with hers. Dianne reacted instantly, lowering her tempo to meet his, her voice leading him back into sync. "There you go. One step at a time. Feel the beat."

She kept her directions light but clear, interspersing her remarks with soft touches to improve his stance. When Chris's steps got more confident, she added a new layer. "Now we're going to add a turn. I'll guide you, don't worry."

She placed her hands on his shoulders, tilting them slightly to signify the direction of the turn. Chris spun awkwardly, his footwork slipping slightly, but Dianne didn't flinch. "Perfect! That's it—just like that," she said, her encouragement genuine. "Let's try it again."

Each iteration produced a slight improvement. Chris started to anticipate the variations in her motions, depending on her tactile clues and verbal instruction to negotiate the pattern. For him, it wasn't just about memorising the steps—it was about developing a relationship, a wordless communication that allowed them to move as one.

> How they built a strong bond of trust and communication from the start.

Mistakes were unavoidable, and there were plenty in those early days. Chris regularly trod on Dianne's toes, misread instructions, or drifted slightly off course. Each time, he whispered an apology, his displeasure clear in the tightness of his voice. But Dianne shook it aside with a giggle, her lightheartedness dispelling the tension.

"You're not the first to stomp on my feet," she laughed after one especially botched spin. "And you definitely won't be the last."

Her humor was disarming, and Chris found himself relaxing in her presence. They began to trade banter during breaks, their chats injecting comedy into the fabric of their performances. "You know," Chris observed one day, wiping perspiration from his brow, "if I can survive this, I might just consider myself invincible."

Dianne grinned. "Invincible, huh? Let's go through the next routine before we start tossing around terms like that."

Their laughing filled the studio, a reminder that even in the midst of hardships, there was joy to be found.

*The unique methods they used to teach choreography without sight.*

Traditional techniques of teaching choreography wouldn't work for Chris. Dianne immediately noticed this and began inventing inventive strategies to bridge the gap. For arm motions, she adopted a hands-on technique, tracing the route of his arms with her own. "Feel this," she'd remark, leading his hand along the arc of a move. "That's the shape we're going for."

For footwork, she touched his feet softly with hers to signify the direction of each step. "Left foot forward, right foot back," she'd yell out, her voice calm and regular. "Now pivot. Good—like that."

When they met especially tough sections, Dianne divided them down into smaller chunks. She utilised a combination of vocal orders and physical clues, repeating each portion until it became second nature. "Think of it like building blocks," she continued. "One piece at a time."

She also presented creative strategies to assist Chris absorb the moves. For one sequence, she put a lightweight resistance band around their waists, allowing Chris to feel the direction of her motions more immediately. "This is just to help you get the flow," she added, her tone encouraging. "Once you've got it, we'll ditch the band."

The approaches weren't flawless, and progress was slow at times. But each modest triumph seemed monumental—a tribute to their mutual dedication and flexibility.

## BREAKTHROUGH

The moment it all began to click occurred during their first complete routine. The music was a spirited cha-cha, its buoyant speed filling the studio with enthusiasm. Chris stood in place, his hand softly resting on Dianne's waist. She offered him a comforting squeeze. "You've got this," she continued, her voice calm.

As the music swelled, they began to move. Chris followed Dianne's lead, his steps timid but deliberate. The rhythm pumped through his body, each beat a guidepost that held him anchored. Dianne's voice sliced through the music, delivering signals and encouragement. "Left. Right. Spin—perfect!"

By the time the final note struck, Chris was exhausted, his chest heaving with exertion. Dianne threw out a shout, clapped her hands together. "You did it!" she shouted, flinging her arms around him. "That was amazing!"

Chris laughed, his relief evident. "Amazing might be a stretch," he remarked, his voice laced with astonishment. "But it felt... good."

"Good?" Dianne repeated, pretending fury. "That was brilliant, Chris. Absolutely brilliant."

## Chapter 4: Dancing Without Boundaries

The studio lights hummed slightly overhead, their quiet hum mingling with the repetitive scuff of shoes over polished wood. Chris McCausland stood in the midst of the big, empty room, his posture rigid but his look firm. The subtle perfume of varnish lingered in the air, mixed with the earthy aroma of well-worn dancing shoes and the odd whiff of citrus from a cleaning solution. The space itself appeared to throb with potential energy, as if it were holding its breath in anticipation of the day's labour ahead.

Dianne Buswell was already at his side, her motions light and deliberate. She talked in measured tones, her Australian accent lively yet concentrated. "Alright, Chris," she murmured, her voice cutting clearly through the silence. "Today's all about steps and flow. We'll start gently, create some muscle memory, and by the end of this, you'll be flying."

Chris chuckled gently, his fingers lightly grasping hers. "Flying, huh? Let's simply strive to not fall."

### Behind-the-scenes training and the challenges of learning intricate routines.

Learning to dance without sight was a task unlike any Chris had experienced before. Comedy relies on timing, on reading the crowd, on words. Dancing, he rapidly discovered, requires a different type of presence. It was about sensing the beat in his body, trusting his partner's guidance, and navigating a world where accuracy mattered as much as desire.

The first dance they attempted was a cha-cha, its lively, joyous beat a sharp contrast to the methodical movements they drilled. Dianne started by breaking down the movements into their smallest components. "One step back, then two quick steps forward," she instructed, her hands softly moving his shoulders as she spoke.

"It's a quick, sharp movement—almost like a heartbeat."

Chris nodded, focused attentively on her words. He felt the soft pressure of her hands as she positioned him, her touch hard but encouraging. As they went, his feet stumbled, frequently missing the beat or landing awkwardly. Each error sent a bolt of fury through him, an emotion he swiftly concealed with a self-deprecating remark. "Well, if dancing was all about enthusiasm, I'd be nailing this," he remarked, his grin apparent in his voice.

Dianne laughed, but her answer was polite. "You're doing better than you think, Chris. things's not about getting things perfect right immediately. It's about finding your rhythm."

*The role of tactile cues, verbal guidance, and emotional connection in mastering the dances.*

Dianne's teaching methods developed with each routine. She recognised traditional education wouldn't work, so she devised a technique that depended on tactile input and verbal clues. When teaching spins, she placed her hands on his waist, exerting light pressure to lead him through the move. For arm motions, she sketched the line she wanted him to follow, her touch staying just long enough for him to assimilate the shape.

"Let's try that spin again," she remarked one afternoon, her voice calm. She stood behind him, her hands softly resting on his shoulders. "When I press here, you pivot. Keep your feet fixed until I assist you through the turn."

Chris followed her direction, his body tight yet responsive. As they repeated the action, he learnt to trust the pressure of her hands, the tiny variations in her touch that led him. By the fourth attempt, he executed the spin cleanly, his movements flowing and controlled.

"Got it!" Dianne shouted, clapping her hands together. "See? That's what happens when you believe me."

Chris grinned, the strain in his shoulders lessening. "Trust you? Sure. Trust myself? Still working on that."

## VERBAL GUIDANCE AND VISUALIZATION

Verbal training became another crucial element in their armoury. Dianne detailed each action in dramatic detail, constructing a mental picture for Chris to follow. "We're going to step into a box shape," she instructed during a waltz rehearsal. "Think of it like this: forward, to the side, back, and then to the other side. It's like sketching a square with your feet."

Her descriptions were precise and constant, allowing Chris to develop a mental image of the motions. She utilised analogies to simplify complicated sequences, linking processes to common movements or objects. "Pretend you're stepping over a puddle," she added during one especially complicated dance. "That's the kind of lift we need in this step."

For Chris, the mix of physical and verbal coaching formed a foundation he could rely on. Each movement became a sequence of interwoven cues—a squeeze on his shoulder, a word in his ear, a touch on his foot—all working together to guide him through the dance.

**THE EMOTIONAL CONNECTION**
Beyond the mechanical requirements, dance requires an emotional connection that Chris hadn't imagined. Each routine was a tale, a performance that needed vulnerability and sincerity. Dianne advised him to lean into the music, to let the beat dictate not just his movements but his emotions.

One especially tough routine was a rumba, a dance noted for its languid, sensuous moves. Chris tried to achieve the proper mix between accuracy and emotion. "I feel like I'm overthinking it," he acknowledged during a break, wiping perspiration from his brow.

Dianne nodded, her expression serious. "You are," she stated simply. "But that's okay. Let's focus on what the music makes you feel. Forget the steps for a moment—just move with me."

She seized his hands, leading him in a steady sway to the music. There was no choreography, no counting—just the two of them dancing together in beat. Chris closed his eyes, allowing the music wash over him, and for the first time, he felt the dance rather than thinking about it.

"That," Dianne remarked gently as the music faded, "is what we're aiming for."

### How Chris adapted to the intense scrutiny of the judges and live audiences.

As the live concerts approached, the strain rose. Rehearsals got longer and more intense, the stakes mounting with each passing day. Chris could feel the weight of the expectations put on him—not only by the show's producers and viewers but by himself.

The first dress rehearsal was a nerve-wracking event. The studio was converted into a bright stage, its floor shining beneath the glare of innumerable lights. The air hummed with energy, a blend of excitement and tension that was almost palpable. Chris stood in his allotted location, his heart hammering as the music began to play.

Dianne's voice was calm yet forceful when she gave him the initial cue. "Step back—now to the side. Good. Keep going."

The routine started easily, their motions synced despite the pressure. But midway through, Chris tripped on a spin, his foot catching uncomfortably on the floor. He recovered fast, but the error stayed in his thoughts, a shadow that hovered over the rest of the performance.

Afterward, he sat on the edge of the platform, his hands clutched firmly in his lap. "I can't mess up like that in front of a live audience," he continued, his voice low.

Dianne sat alongside him, her tone kind but forceful. "Chris, you're human. Mistakes happen. What counts is how you move on from them."

Her remarks stuck with him as they resumed rehearsals, encouraging him to focus not on perfection but on resilience.

## FACING THE JUDGES

The first live concert was a whirl of music and action. The audience's acclaim exploded in Chris's ears as he took his place on the stage, his hand securely clutching Dianne's. The floor seemed smooth and harsh beneath his boots, the heat of the stage lights leaving a tiny sheen of sweat over his brow.

The music began, and for the next two minutes, Chris threw every ounce of attention and intensity into the routine. He moved in step with Dianne's coaching, his body reacting to her subtle suggestions and the rhythm of the music.

When the final note played, they struck their concluding posture, the audience bursting into cheers.

The judges' remarks were a mixed bag—praise for his commitment and growth, balanced by notes on areas for development. Chris listened closely, his expression impassive, but when the results were disclosed, he couldn't disguise the slight smile that pulled at his lips.

As they departed the stage, Dianne leaned forward, her speech barely heard over the clamour. "You did it," she replied, her pride clear.

Chris nodded, his grasp on her hand tightening. "We did it."

## Chapter 5: The Dance Floor: A New Arena

The dance floor sparkled like polished obsidian beneath the glare of a thousand lights. The air hummed with expectation, a live energy that flared in every corner of the huge studio. Chris McCausland stood at the edge of the stage, his hand resting softly on Dianne's. He could feel the small trembling in her grip—not anxiety, but exhilaration. Beyond the dazzling lights and the rising buzz of the audience, the music technician's final tweaks transmitted faint echoes over the huge area.

Chris inclined his head slightly, letting the noises settle around him, anchoring himself. The audience's talk felt like waves, rising and dropping in sync. Somewhere among them were his wife and children, their applause interlaced into the noise. But now, they were simply a haze in his memory. His attention focused to the stage beneath his feet, Dianne by his side, and the pulse of the music ready to begin.

"You ready?" Dianne murmured, bending in just enough for her voice to reach him above the hum of the throng. Her voice, firm and loving, grounded him.

Chris breathed gently, his lips twisting into a sardonic smile. "Ready as I'll ever be."

**Highlights from Chris's first few performances.**

The initial notes of their routine exploded from the speakers, a cha-cha rhythm that pumped with joyous intensity. Chris tightened his grasp on Dianne's hand as they started onto the first stairs. The world around them appeared to dissolve, leaving only the music, her words, and the mild, tactile instruction she provided with each motion.

"Step forward—two quick steps back," she said just loud enough for him to hear. Her touch directed him with exquisite precision, a squeeze on his shoulder here, a tiny movement of her fingers there.

The motions felt clumsy at first. His mind raced to keep up with the sequence, the weight transfers, the rotations. But as the pattern proceeded, a weird thing began to happen. His body started to respond by instinct, the rhythm cementing itself in his muscles. The audience's applause surged at important times, their enthusiasm a physical wave that drove him forward.

When the final note landed, they struck their concluding pose—Chris somewhat winded, his chest heaving from the strain. For a minute, the stillness that followed was deafening. Then the crowd exploded, their shouts echoing through the studio. Chris could feel the vibrations of their applauding through the floor beneath his feet, a feeling that sent a shudder rushing up his spine.

Dianne drew him into a swift hug, her voice brimming with pride. "You did it! We did it!"

He gave out a weak laugh, his grin broadening. "I didn't fall. I'll regard that as a win."

*The emotional rollercoaster of rehearsals, mistakes, and triumphs.*

Rehearsals for their following appearances brought with them a whole new set of obstacles. The routines got increasingly difficult, the moves needing greater accuracy and synchronisation. For Chris, the voyage was a continuous test of focus, trust, and resilience. Each slip seemed like a minor failure, each stumble a reminder of how far he still had to go.

One especially demanding practice had him seated on the studio floor, his back against the mirrored wall. Sweat streamed down his temples, his hands resting heavy on his knees. Dianne crouched in front of him, her demeanour serene yet resolute.

"You're overthinking again," she observed, offering him a bottle of water. "You're trying to dance with your head instead of your body."

Chris shook his head, his displeasure visible in the tightness of his jaw. "I just... I can't seem to get it properly. It's like my head understands what to do, but my feet haven't gotten the memo."

Dianne stretched out, resting a hand on his shoulder. "You're doing better than you think, Chris. You've got the steps. Now let's focus on how it feels. Trust me, okay?"

Her reassurance was a lifeline, drawing him back from the edge of self-doubt. They repeated the exercise again, and though it wasn't flawless, each effort pushed him closer to understanding the sequence.

## TRIUMPHS ON THE FLOOR

Their second performance was a quickstep, its vibrant tempo a dramatic contrast to the more controlled rhythm of their previous routine. The music rose, filling the studio with a buoyant spirit that echoed the crowd's delight. Chris walked with renewed confidence, his steps lighter, his motions more certain.

The sequence was replete with precise footwork and quick twists, each one needing split-second timing. Dianne's vocal hints helped him through the most tough portions, her voice calm and regular. "Quick, quick—slow. And pivot. Beautiful!"

By the time they reached the last posture, the audience was on its feet, their applause a thunderous clamour. Chris felt a flush of pride that briefly eclipsed his tiredness. He turned to Dianne, his grin broad. "I think we nailed that one."

She chuckled, slinging her arm around his shoulders. "You didn't just nail it—you smashed it."

*Fan reactions, audience support, and growing public affection for Chris.*

As the weeks went on, Chris began to observe a difference in the audience's emotions. What had begun as polite applause evolved became full-throated yells, their joy engulfing the room like a tidal wave. The support went beyond the live shows—messages flooded in on social media, people sharing their respect for his boldness, his humor, and his resolve.

"I watched your performance with my daughter," one message said. "She's blind, and seeing you out there made her believe she can do anything."

Chris read the messages with a mix of humility and surprise. He hadn't set out to inspire anyone—he was just trying to keep up with Dianne's steps and live each week. But knowing his tale connected with individuals brought a new depth of importance to his time on the show.

**FACING THE JUDGES**

The judges' remarks were a continual source of tension and drive. Some gave positive input, applauding his development while pointing out areas for growth. Others were less forgiving, their words piercing into his confidence like a sword.

After one especially stinging review, Chris sat in the green room, his hands tightly gripped together. Dianne joined him, her countenance a combination of irritation and resolve.

"They don't see what I see," she replied firmly. "They don't see the work you've put in, the progress you've made. And that's their loss. You simply keep doing what you're doing."

Her comments sparked the fire in him, reminding him why he was there—not for the judges, but for himself, for Dianne, and for everyone who believed in him.

**GROWING PUBLIC AFFECTION**

By the midway of the tournament, Chris had become a fan favorite. Viewers identified with his humor, his vulnerability, and his relentless persistence. They cheered for him not simply as a dancer but as a symbol of perseverance and promise.

On performance evenings, the excitement in the studio was tremendous. Fans put up placards displaying his name, their applause booming long after the music stopped. Chris sensed their support in every stride he took, their belief in him driving his own.

**THE JOURNEY FORWARD**

Each week offered new difficulties, new routines, and new opportunity to improve. Chris embraced the highs and lows with a tenacity that encouraged everyone around him. The dance floor, once a strange and scary environment, had become a platform where he could not only perform but flourish.

And as the competition proceeded, one thing became clear: Chris McCausland wasn't simply dancing—he was shattering limits, one step at a time.

## Chapter 6: The Glitterball Dream

The air in the studio seemed thick with expectancy, the type that poured into every corner and wrapped itself around the candidates like an unseen cloak. Chris McCausland stood at the edge of the dance floor, the familiar hum of the lights overhead forming a gentle background beat to the enthusiastic whispers of the audience beyond the stage. He altered his stance, shaking out his arms while Dianne Buswell stood alongside him, her hand resting softly on his arm.

"We've got this," she murmured, her voice firm, her energies emanating a peaceful assurance.

Chris let out a deep breath, nodding. The music was cued, the judges poised at their table, pencils in hand, and the spotlight focused onto the polished floor where their feet would soon be moving in tandem. This wasn't just another performance. Tonight, the stakes felt higher. It wasn't merely about the steps or the time. It was about every moment that had gotten him here, the result of weeks of struggle, sweat, and commitment.

### The pivotal moments in the competition that defined Chris's journey.

One of the most significant moments in Chris's journey came during a contemporary routine aimed to express a highly personal tale. The composition was put to a hauntingly lovely tune, its notes weaving a feeling of melancholy and optimism. Dianne had choreographed it with Chris's life in mind, each movement signifying a chapter of his journey—his upbringing, his loss of sight, and his fortitude in the face of hardship.

The studio was hushed when the music began. Chris moved gingerly at first, his movements deliberate as he listened to Dianne's subtle verbal signals and followed the gentle touches she made on his shoulders or arms to lead him. But as the routine unfolded, something altered. The choreography needed an emotional rawness that pushed Chris beyond his comfort zone. It wasn't just about performing the moves; it was about embracing them, letting his tale flow through his body like an unwritten language.

By the time the final note faded, Chris and Dianne were holding their finishing stance, their breathing evident in the silence that followed. For a minute, there was no sound save the gentle buzz of the lights. Then the audience burst into applause, their cheers surging like a tsunami that slammed over the stage.

Backstage, Chris slumped against the wall, still recovering his breath. "That was… something," he continued, his voice tinted with wonder.

Dianne grinned, her fingers grasping his arm strongly. "It wasn't just something, Chris. It was everything."

The judges mirrored her perspective, their remarks overflowing with appreciation. "Tonight, you didn't just dance," one of them observed, their tone overflowing with adoration. "You moved us. You told a narrative, and it was unforgettable."

*Key performances that earned high praise from the judges and fans.*

Weeks later, Chris found himself attempting a samba, a dance famed for its intricacy and strong intensity. The cheerful music pumped through the studio as he and Dianne rehearsed, their motions interrupted by bursts of laughter as he faltered through the precise footwork.

"This is impossible," Chris grumbled after his fifth failed effort at a particularly tough step.

Dianne shook her head, her voice strong yet encouraging. "It's not impossible. It's samba. It's intended to feel chaotic. Embrace it."

The night of the concert, the vibe in the studio was electrifying. The samba was a riot of color and movement, its rhythm irresistible. Chris launched himself into the drill, his steps less exact but filled with passion. The crowd's chants got louder with every turn, their enthusiasm pulling him onwards.

When the song stopped, he struck the final position, a huge grin on his face as the audience yelled their approbation. The judges complimented his commitment, applauding his ability to convey the essence of the samba even if the technique wasn't immaculate.

"Chris," one judge added with a smile, "you remind us that dance isn't just about perfection. It's about joy. And tonight, you brought us joy."

The Argentine Tango: A Testament to Trust
Another defining moment came with the Argentine tango, a dance that needed accuracy, passion, and an almost telepathic connection between couples. The dance was powerful, its motions quick and methodical, each step requiring a degree of synchronisation that left Chris feeling both thrilled and daunted.

Dianne spent hours working with him to master the technique. She guided him through the complicated footwork, her touch firm and steady as she led him through the sharp pivots and dramatic pauses. "This dance is about control," she remarked after a break. "It's not just about the steps—it's about the tension, the push and pull between us."

On performance night, the stage was flooded in deep crimson light, the atmosphere packed with expectation. Chris felt the weight of the occasion as the music began, its mournful tune establishing the tone. He walked with a focus that bordered on intensity, each stride thoughtful, each action a reflection of the trust he'd developed with Dianne.

By the time they finished, the studio was hushed for a beat before bursting into applause. The judges' remarks were wonderful, their praise stressing the bond between Chris and Dianne that had brought the routine to life.

### The significance of each routine beyond the technical execution.

As the competition advanced, each routine took on a meaning that transcended beyond the technical performance. For Chris, dancing had become a channel for expression, a method to share what words couldn't quite describe. Every performance was a mirror of his journey—a monument to tenacity, determination, and the power of human connection.

During one rehearsal, Dianne said something that remained with him. "You're not just learning to dance, Chris. You're telling folks that it's good to venture into the unknown, to take chances and appreciate the process."

Her remarks resonated deeply, moulding his attitude to each new issue. He began to see dancing not as a goal to accomplish but as a method to push boundaries, to show to himself and others that limitations were designed to be transcended.

## FAN REACTIONS AND GROWING SUPPORT

As Chris's performances continued to enchant audiences, the outpouring of support from fans swelled. Messages rushed in, each one a witness to the influence his trip had on individuals from all walks of life.

"Watching you dance has been the highlight of my week," one fan said. "You remind us all that anything is possible."

The messages spurred Chris's motivation, reminding him that his trip wasn't just about the competition. It was about the relationships he was building, the inspiration he was offering, and the obstacles he was helping to shatter.

## THE GLITTERBALL DREAM

The closer they went to the climax, the more the fantasy of the Glitterball Trophy felt within grasp. Each performance took them one step closer, each rehearsal a reminder of how far they'd come. Chris and Dianne poured their souls into every routine, their friendship becoming deeper with each hurdle they overcame.

On the night of the finale, the studio was alive with expectation. The atmosphere buzzed with intensity, the crowd's applause reverberating through the arena as Chris and Dianne took their positions for their last performance. The routine was a culmination of all they'd learned, a dance that embodied their trip in every stride, every turn, every pulse.

When the final note played and the crowd burst into applause, Chris stood in the center of the floor, his chest heaving with effort, a proud smile on his face. For him, the trip had never been about the prize. It had been about the development, the friendships, and the moments that had characterised his time on the dance floor.

## Chapter 7: Breaking Barriers, Changing Perceptions

The air outside the studio was brisk with the sting of late October, a startling contrast to the warmth indoors. The glow of television lights and the murmur of expectancy filled the auditorium, an atmosphere both exciting and weighty with significance. Chris McCausland waited in the wings, waiting for his cue, the familiar feel of Dianne Buswell's hand delicately resting on his forearm. Her touch was calming, a continuous presence in a world that had evolved into an arena of obstacles he could never have foreseen.

The ovation from the previous section still rang, a reminder of the audience's passion for what Strictly Come Dancing represented—an mix of elegance, grit, and entertainment. But for Chris, this adventure had transcended the stage. It wasn't only about perfecting routines or winning scores. It was about altering a story that has been engraved into society's collective mentality for far too long.

### How Chris's success on *Strictly Come Dancing* challenged societal norms about disability and ability.

Chris's journey on Strictly was considerably more than a personal success; it was a disturbance to long-standing notions about ability. For years, popular conceptions of blindness were connected to limitation—a constant focus on what couldn't be done. Chris, however, had spun that theory on its head. His appearance on the dance floor wasn't simply unexpected—it was revolutionary.

From the very first week, the murmuring began. Critics and observers worried if it was even viable for someone without sight to participate in a sport so strongly based in visual acuity. "How can he possibly follow choreography?" some questioned. "How will he keep pace with a partner, or match the rhythm of the music?"

These doubts weren't malevolent, but they were ingrained in a viewpoint that had yet to be addressed.

Chris's performances were the solution. Each routine emerged as a monument to adaptation and trust, a clear display of how limits might be reframed. The first time he and Dianne completed a faultless turn in the quickstep, the crowd burst into applause—not merely for the technical performance but for what it meant. Chris was moving in tune with the music, with his partner, with the intensity of the moment, directed not by sight but by an unyielding drive and an unshakeable bond.

## BREAKING THE SILENCE AROUND DISABILITY

As the weeks passed, Chris's narrative became a focal point of debates well beyond the Strictly stage. Media sources covered his development with a mix of astonishment and curiosity. Interviews dug into his techniques, his problems, and his accomplishments. But more crucially, they began to throw a light on the greater story of disability in the public eye.

Chris never shied away from the matter. In press rooms and post-show interviews, he spoke openly about the problems he faced—not only on the dance floor, but in navigating a society that sometimes misjudged him. "It's not about proving people wrong," he stated during one interview, his voice calm. "It's about showing them what's possible when you approach things differently."

His remarks resonated strongly. They weren't just about him—they were about the millions of individuals living with disabilities who had been caged into preconceived assumptions of what they could or couldn't achieve. Chris's journey became a bridge, linking his personal experience to a bigger discourse about representation and inclusion.

**THE PUBLIC RESPONSE**

The response from fans was phenomenal. Messages flooded in, each one a witness to the impact Chris was making on people's lives. Parents of blind children wrote to explain how his performances had motivated their youngsters to dream larger, to see possibilities where others saw difficulties. Viewers with disabilities remarked how his trip had given them hope and recognition, a reminder that they, too, deserved to take up a place in the world.

One message in particular resonated with Chris. A young woman wrote, "I've spent my whole life being told I couldn't do things because of my disability. Watching you dance, I realized I've been asking the incorrect question. It's not 'Can I do this?' It's 'How can I make it work?' Thank you for showing me that."

Chris read each note with a mix of humility and wonder. For him, this was never about being a role model—it was about showing up, doing the job, and letting the results speak for themselves.

But the outpouring of solidarity was overwhelming. It was a tribute to the appetite for stories that questioned the status quo and embraced perseverance in all its manifestations.

> The impact of his journey on the broader conversation around representation in entertainment.

Chris's participation on Strictly Come Dancing prompted a bigger conversation about representation in the entertainment business. For years, disability had been overlooked, frequently reduced to tokenism or depicted via stereotypes. Chris's appearance on a prime-time platform provided a counterbalance to that narrative. He wasn't there as a curiosity or an exception—he was there as a competitor, an equal, a partner.

Producers and creatives began to take notice. The principle of inclusion wasn't new, but Chris's path emphasised its relevance in a manner that couldn't be ignored. His performances weren't only about technical proficiency; they were about honesty. He wasn't attempting to fit into a mold—he was changing it totally.

For spectators, witnessing Chris succeed on the dance floor wasn't just inspiring—it was normalizing. Each week, he became less of a novelty and more of a fixture, someone who belonged not in spite of his blindness, but because of his ability, determination, and humanity. His presence reminded viewers that representation wasn't about ticking a box—it was about establishing venues where everyone could see themselves represented.

**THE POWER OF PARTNERSHIP**
At the core of Chris's adventure was his collaboration with Dianne Buswell. Their connection went beyond the mechanics of dance—it was a lesson in communication, trust, and cooperation. Every stride they took was a monument to the strength of their friendship, a reminder that success was never a single venture.

Their routines weren't just performances—they were talks. Each movement communicated a tale of adaptability and perseverance, of two individuals traversing unfamiliar ground together. For Chris, Dianne's unshakeable conviction in his potential was a lifeline. For Dianne, Chris's resolve was a source of inspiration.

Audiences recognised the sincerity of their connection, and it became a cornerstone of the show's storyline. They weren't simply dancing—they were tearing down walls, one stride at a time.

**CHANGING PERCEPTIONS**
By the time the tournament entered its final weeks, the discussion around Chris had transformed. No longer was the focus on whether he could dance—it was on how he performed, on the originality and emotion he brought to each routine. The judges applauded his ability to connect with the audience, to

express tales via movement in a way that exceeded technical accuracy.

For Chris, the influence of his adventure stretched far beyond the Glitterball Trophy. It was in the notes from fans, the debates started by his performances, and the shifts in perception that reverberated out from the dance floor into the world beyond.

**A LEGACY OF POSSIBILITY**

As the final chords of his last performance played and the ovation rang around him, Chris stood in the center of the stage, Dianne by his side. He couldn't see the dazzling confetti dropping from above or the tears in the eyes of the crowd, but he could sense the weight of the occasion. It wasn't just about winning—it was about all they had achieved together, the barriers they had broken, the tales they had told.

## Chapter 8: Triumph and Heartache: The Emotional Journey

The studio was unnaturally still when the cameras stopped rolling, the loud ovation of the live audience remaining only as a faint murmur in Chris McCausland's ears. He stood at the edge of the dance floor, his breathing hard, his palms moist with sweat. Dianne Buswell was by his side, her hand resting softly on his arm, the smallest touch of her fingers stabilising him among the whirl of emotions.

They had just concluded their third performance of the season, a rumba that needed more vulnerability than any dance Chris had performed previously. The routine had gone smoothly—at least, that's what Dianne had informed him. But Chris couldn't shake the strain in his chest, a persistent uncertainty that said he could have done better.

"Breathe," Dianne whispered calmly, her voice firm and serene. "You did everything we worked on. Let it go."

Chris nodded, swallowing the knot in his throat. He knew she was correct, but it didn't relieve the weight weighing down on him. This wasn't simply about getting the steps correct. It was about demonstrating to himself that he belonged here, on this stage, in this world.

*The highs and lows of Chris's time on *Strictly Come Dancing*.*

There were moments when the strain melted away, when everything clicked, and Chris felt an indisputable feeling of triumph. One of those instances occurred during their salsa performance, a fast-paced, high-energy dance that stretched his boundaries in ways he hadn't imagined.

Rehearsals for the salsa had been tough. The beat was unrelenting, the steps sophisticated, and the lifts needed power and technique Chris wasn't sure he possessed. But Dianne believed in him, her encouragement unflinching.

"Trust your instincts," she had advised during their final practice, her voice hard yet kind. "You've got this."

On the night of the performance, when the music burst from the speakers, Chris pushed himself into the routine with everything he had. The crowd's cheers mixed with the music, a wall of sound that propelled him onwards. Each turn, each lift, each stride seemed like a little success, a rejection of the worries that had haunted him before.

When they struck their final posture, Chris was exhausted, his chest heaving with exertion. The clamour of the audience flowed over him, and for the first time, he allowed himself to feel the weight of their support.

Dianne put her arms around him, her laughter bursting over with joy. "You smashed it!" she shouted, her excitement contagious.

Chris grinned, his voice weak with passion. "We smashed it."

*Personal moments of doubt, growth, and discovery.*

But for every high, there were lows that strained Chris's commitment. One especially trying week came a foxtrot that left him feeling absolutely devastated. The delicacy and accuracy of the dance seemed beyond his grasp, the exquisite footwork evading him at every turn.

By the conclusion of their second practice, Chris was sitting on the studio floor, his head in his hands. Sweat trickled down his brow, settling in the hollow of his collarbone. Dianne knelt alongside him, her look a mixture of compassion and resolve.

"You're putting too much pressure on yourself," she replied gently. "It's not about being perfect. It's about connecting with the dance, with the music, with me."

Chris shook his head, his irritation spilling up. "But what if that's not enough? What if I just can't do it?"

Dianne placed a hand on his shoulder, her grasp tight. "You can do it, Chris. I know you can. You've shown it to me every single week."

Her comments stuck with him, resonating in his head as they resumed the pattern. It wasn't an immediate breakthrough—there were still blunders, moments of doubt—but by the time they reached performance night, Chris had discovered a rhythm that carried him through. The dance wasn't great, but it was sincere, and the crowd responded with a standing ovation.

## DISCOVERING STRENGTH

As the competition proceeded, Chris began to unearth reservoirs of power he hadn't realised he possessed. Each practice pushed him further, demanding more from his body, his mind, and his spirit. The physical toll was undeniable—aches and pains that remained long after rehearsals ended—but it was the emotional voyage that left the greatest impression.

During one especially hard week, Chris confided in Dianne about the weight he was bearing. "It's not just about the dancing," he said, his voice subdued. "It's about what it represents. For myself, for my family, for everyone who's watching and rooting for me. It's a lot."

Dianne nodded, her expression serious. "It is a lot," she remarked. "But you don't have to carry it alone. We're a team, Chris. We've got this together."

Her statements were a turning moment. Chris recognised that he didn't have to face the load of expectation on his own. He had Dianne, his family, the audience, and a growing group of supporters who believed in him.

> The profound emotional impact of his journey on Chris and those around him.

The influence of Chris's adventure reached well beyond the dance floor. His performances connected with people in ways he hadn't imagined, generating debates about resilience, representation, and the value of venturing outside one's comfort zone.

Messages flooded in from people who saw themselves in Chris's experience. "Watching you dance has been the highlight of my week," one commented. "You've shown me that it's okay to be vulnerable, to try something new, even if it scares you."

For Chris, these comments were both humbling and empowering. They reminded him of the ripple effect of his path, the way it was motivating people to overcome their own obstacles and embrace their potential.

## THE FINAL WEEKS: A MIX OF JOY AND SADNESS

As the tournament reached its finale, the emotional stakes were higher. Each performance seemed like a farewell, a melancholy reminder that this great trip was nearing an end. Chris pushed everything into the last exercises, aiming to leave nothing on the floor.

The conclusion was a flurry of emotions. The studio was alive with excitement, the crowd's chants thunderous as Chris and Dianne prepared for their last dance. The routine was a culmination of all they had learnt together, a celebration of the friendship they had made and the obstacles they had broken.

When the final note struck and the audience burst into applause, Chris stood in the center of the floor, his chest heaving, his face moist with perspiration and tears. He couldn't see the dazzling confetti dropping from above, but he could feel the love and pride flowing from every corner of the room.

Dianne held him hard, her voice shaking with sorrow. "You did it, Chris. You truly did it."

Chris smiled, his voice strangled with thanks. "We did it."

## Chapter 9: The Final Dance: Victory Beyond the Glitterball

The studio was alive with expectation. Rows of chairs were filled with cheering spectators, their voices blending into an electric buzz that vibrated through the polished hardwood floor. Overhead, lights glittered like tiny stars, creating a golden glow over the huge ballroom scene. The air was thick with expectancy, a mix of excitement and tension that wrapped itself around every candidate waiting in the wings.

Chris McCausland stood just inside the curtain, his hands relaxed at his sides, his breathing steady but purposeful. Beside him, Dianne Buswell adjusted the border of her sequined dress, her gestures light but precise, her attention steadfast. She placed her hand on his arm, a delicate squeeze that gave a silent word of support.

"This is it," she said, her voice low yet forceful. "This is what we've worked for."

Chris nodded, his lips curling into a slight grin. He could feel the adrenaline flowing through his veins, a heady mix of nerves and ecstasy. It wasn't simply another performance. This was the climax, the culmination of months of arduous practices, soaring successes, and times of doubt. The Glitterball Trophy was within sight, but for Chris, the stakes felt considerably greater. This wasn't just about winning—it was about everything the journey had come to signify.

*The moment Chris and Dianne won the Glitterball Trophy.*

The announcer's voice boomed through the studio, introducing their final performance with an enthusiasm that sent a ripple of applause through the crowd. Chris and Dianne stepped onto the stage together, the floor beneath their feet familiar yet daunting. The scent of fresh flowers arranged around the judges' table mingled with the faint tang of stage lights warming the air.

The music began softly, a haunting melody that swelled with emotion. Chris stood tall, his posture poised, his focus entirely on Dianne's subtle cues. She placed his hand on her waist, guiding him into the first step. Their movements were fluid, each turn and lift imbued with the weight of their shared journey.

Every moment felt alive, charged with energy and meaning. The routine wasn't just a performance—it was a story, one they had written together with every stumble, every laugh, every late-night rehearsal that stretched into exhaustion. As they danced, the crowd's cheers faded into the background, replaced by the rhythm of the music and the quiet trust that had grown between them.

By the time they reached the final pose, Chris was breathless, his chest heaving with exertion. Dianne wrapped her arms around him, her laughter bubbling with relief and joy. The audience erupted into applause, the sound cascading over them like a wave. Chris could feel the vibrations through the floor, a tactile reminder of the support that had carried them this far.

## THE ANNOUNCEMENT

The tension in the studio was palpable as the hosts gathered the contestants on the stage. Chris and Dianne stood shoulder to shoulder, their hands clasped tightly, their breaths synchronized as they waited for the final announcement. The Glitterball Trophy gleamed under the spotlight, a dazzling reminder of what was at stake.

The seconds stretched into what felt like an eternity. Chris could hear the faint creak of the microphone as the host raised it to her lips, the rustle of fabric as the contestants shifted in anticipation. Then, with a flourish, the winner was announced.

"Chris and Dianne!"

The words hit like a thunderclap, the crowd erupting into cheers so loud they seemed to shake the room. Chris froze for a moment, the reality of the announcement sinking in like a wave crashing over him. Dianne let out a joyful cry, pulling him into a tight embrace.

"You did it!" she exclaimed, her voice trembling with emotion. "We did it!"

Chris laughed, the sound raw and unrestrained. "I can't believe it," he said, his voice barely audible over the roar of the crowd. "We actually did it."

## THE TROPHY PRESENTATION

As they were guided to the center of the stage, the Glitterball Trophy was handed to them, its reflective surface catching the light in a dazzling display. Chris held it carefully, the weight of the moment heavier than the trophy itself. The cheers of the crowd surrounded them, a wall of sound that seemed to amplify every emotion coursing through him.

He felt Dianne's hand on his shoulder, steadying him as he raised the trophy. The applause swelled, the energy in the room almost tangible. It wasn't just about the win—it was about everything the trophy represented. For Chris, it was a symbol of resilience, of pushing beyond boundaries and redefining what was possible.

*Reflections on what the victory meant to Chris and the disability community.*

Later that night, in the quiet minutes following the celebration, Chris sat backstage, the trophy laying next to him. The adrenaline had dissipated, leaving behind a tremendous sense of accomplishment. Dianne sat next to him, her energy still intense, but her voice was lower now.

"Do you realize what you've done?" she questioned, her tone filled with wonder. "This isn't just about Glitterball, Chris. You've revolutionised how others view what's possible."

Chris shook his head, a slight smile flickering on his lips. "I didn't do it alone," he remarked simply. "You were with me every step of the way."

**THE BROADER IMPACT**

The triumph wasn't simply a personal milestone—it was an event that resonated well beyond the dance floor. For the handicap community, Chris's path had been a beacon of hope and representation. Messages rushed in from individuals around the country, their messages filled with thanks and encouragement.

"You've shown me that my blindness doesn't define me," one message said. "If you can do this, I can take on anything."

For Chris, the messages were humbling. They reminded him that the actual success lay not in the trophy but in the lives he had touched, the conversations he had ignited, and the barriers he had helped to shatter.

*How the win became a symbol of determination, resilience, and the power of inclusivity.*

The Glitterball Trophy became more than a prize—it became a symbol of inclusion and the strength of resolve. Chris's success prompted the entertainment business to reassess its approach to representation, showing that talent and persistence could shine through any impediment.

Producers and viewers alike began to think on the tales they chose to portray and the voices they amplified. Chris's path wasn't simply a success story—it was a call to action, a reminder that inclusion wasn't a surrender but a celebration of difference.

## THE LEGACY OF THE FINAL DANCE

As Chris prepared to leave the studio for the last time, the weight of his trip weighed over him. He couldn't see the confetti that still covered the floor or the way the lights threw long shadows across the now-empty stage. But he could feel the warmth of Dianne's presence alongside him, the steady cadence of her steps matching his as they moved toward the exit.

For Chris, the triumph wasn't an endpoint—it was a beginning. It was a reminder that diving into the unknown, no matter how intimidating, may lead to something spectacular. And when he held the Glitterball Trophy one more time before placing it carefully in its case, he couldn't help but grin.

This was more than a win. It was a message, a tale, and a spark that would continue to light the path for those to follow.

## Chapter 10: Legacy of a Champion

The morning following the Strictly Come Dancing finale was both quieter and noisier than Chris McCausland had envisioned. The silence came in the moments before morning, as he sat in his living room, the faint creak of his beloved recliner anchoring him in the stillness. The Glitterball Trophy rested on the coffee table, its shiny surface capturing the faint glimmer of the early sun. He couldn't see it, but he stroked his fingertips over its cold, smooth surface, tracing the complex patterns engraved into the base.

The volume came later—text messages pinging ceaselessly, his phone buzzing on the table as friends, family, and admirers rushed him with congratulations. Social media was alive with hashtags displaying his name, his journey, and the sense of pride his win had generated in many others. Headlines portrayed him as a trailblazer, a game-changer, someone who had redefined what it meant to push limits. Yet for Chris, it all seemed unreal.

**Chris's life after *Strictly Come Dancing*: how the experience reshaped his career and public image.**

The weeks after the finale were a frenzy. Chris found himself managing a new type of attention, one that extended beyond his comic profession. Offers flooded in—from interviews and panel programs to documentaries and speaking engagements. Everyone appeared anxious to learn more about the man who had not only danced his way into the hearts of millions but had also transformed preconceptions about ability and representation.

Chris addressed the rush of offers with his trademark humor and groundedness. At one interview, a host asked him whether he ever believed he'd be holding the Glitterball Trophy when he first stepped onto the Strictly stage. He chuckled, his voice warm and self-effacing. "I didn't imagine I'd still be standing, let alone holding a trophy. But I think life has a way of surprising you."

Comedy remained his cornerstone, but his performances began to develop. His experiences on Strictly poured into his act, bringing a fresh depth of narrative that resonated emotionally with viewers. He laughed about his earliest efforts at dancing, about Dianne's tolerance, and about the ridiculousness of attempting to learn a tango while secretly wishing he wouldn't trip. But underneath the laughter was something more—a sense of introspection, a knowledge of how far he had come and how much he had learned.

**SHAPING THE CONVERSATION**
Chris's trip on Strictly had generated a discourse that reached well beyond the dance floor. Media sources proceeded to investigate the themes of his tale, diving into the value of representation in entertainment and the ways his success had defied conventional conventions. But it wasn't only journalists who were talking—viewers from

many walks of life were connecting with the bigger implications of his journey.

Messages flooded in from people who saw themselves in Chris's experience. A student with a mobility limitation wrote about how witnessing him dance had motivated her to apply for her school's theatrical play. A father of two blind children explained how Chris's win had given his family hope and a renewed feeling of potential. "You showed them," the letter said, "that they don't have to sit on the sidelines."

For Chris, these words were humbling and extremely personal. He frequently spent hours replying to them, his comments carefully crafted to praise the courage and tenacity of individuals who had sought out. Each letter reinforced the impression that his trip had become a communal experience, one that went well beyond the bounds of a television program.

*The lasting influence of his journey on the entertainment industry and viewers alike.*

Behind the scenes, Chris's effect was spreading across the entertainment business. Producers and networks began to reconsider their approach to casting and storytelling, realising the need for more inclusive tales that represented the different reality of their consumers.

Chris's accomplishment provided a roadmap, a reminder that authenticity and representation weren't simply buzzwords—they were important to create meaningful, relevant material. He was invited to participate in panels and seminars geared at increasing diversity in the arts, where his comments bore the weight of lived experience.

"People aren't looking for perfection," he stated during one debate. "They're looking for connection. They want to witness tales that represent their own hardships, their own achievements. And if we're not communicating those tales, we're missing the point."

*How Chris continues to advocate for inclusivity, visibility, and empowerment.*

As his reputation evolved, Chris became an advocate for diversity and visibility, utilising his voice to magnify debates around disability and representation. He worked with groups focussing on accessibility and inclusion, providing his support to efforts aimed at breaking down barriers in education, employment, and the arts.

One of his most influential ventures was a campaign that showcased the achievements of persons with disabilities across numerous disciplines. The ad included human tales, each one a monument to persistence and ingenuity. Chris's engagement wasn't just about contributing his name—it was about establishing a forum where these tales could be shared and honoured.

"I'm not the first person to push against expectations," he stated during the campaign's launch event. "And I won't be the last. But if my experience helps open a door for someone else, then it's all been worth it."

**REFLECTIONS ON CHANGE**

In calmer moments, Chris often thought about the influence of his Strictly experience—not just on his profession but on his sense of self. The experience had pushed him to address anxieties, to embrace vulnerability, and to trust in the process of progress. It had told him that strength wasn't about perfection; it was about tenacity, about turning up even when the odds were impossible.

For Chris, the Glitterball Trophy wasn't only a sign of success. It was a reminder of the power of teamwork, of the link he had created with Dianne, and of the numerous individuals who had supported him along the road. It was a monument to the belief that going into the unknown may lead to something exceptional.

## CONCLUSION

The stage was dark now, bereft of the bright lights and the swirl of applause that had previously marked Chris McCausland's journey on Strictly Come Dancing. The wooden floor, polished to a smooth sheen, bore subtle scuff marks—ghosts of innumerable rehearsals, moments of success, and the occasional misstep. Chris stood in the centre of the quiet studio, his hand resting softly on the barre, his thoughts reliving the cadence of routines long gone danced. The echoes of his laughing with Dianne, the directions screamed over music, and the shouts of an audience that had loved him seemed to remain in the air.

In the calm, there was clarity. Chris had entered into Strictly with no aspirations beyond attempting something new, exploring the boundaries of his comfort zone. But what he had found—on the dance floor, in the friendships he created, and in the hearts of those who followed his journey—was far better than a trophy or acclaim. It was a reminder of what might happen when fear gave way to bravery, when faith conquered doubt, and when the human spirit refused to settle for anything less than spectacular.

> A reflection on Chris's journey and the ongoing message of hope and perseverance.

Chris's narrative was never simply about dancing. From the minute he took that first timid step onto the dance floor, it became a tale of optimism, one that went well beyond his personal experience. Each fall, each mistake, and each accomplishment spoke to the common struggles of self-doubt and the constant search of progress. His journey was not defined by perfection but by tenacity, a trait that connected powerfully with everybody who had ever faced their own uphill trek.

During rehearsals, there were innumerable instances when the steps felt insurmountable. An error here, a missed beat there, the frustration of not being able to rely on sight to anticipate his next move—it might have been unbearable. But Chris's determination never wavered. With Dianne's instruction and an uncompromising determination, he pushed through the anxiety and frustration, learning to trust his instincts and the rhythm of his body. In the process, he discovered a strength he hadn't realised he possessed—a quiet resilience that carried him through every performance and beyond.

Offstage, this drive translated into a message that resonated with millions. Chris's tale wasn't simply inspiring—it was empowering. It taught people that difficulty wasn't the end of the road, but the start of a new journey, one full with opportunity and discovery.

*Final thoughts on the broader impact of his story and how it continues to inspire people worldwide.*

Chris's journey on Strictly Come Dancing didn't simply captivate the hearts of spectators in his own nation. It flowed outward, reaching audiences throughout the globe. Social media became a hotbed of debates about his performances, with admirers sharing video, memories, and comments on what his trip had meant to them. His acts were more than entertainment—they were assertions of possibility, proof that walls were supposed to be shattered.

One communication came from a teenager in Brazil, who had been blind since birth. "Watching you dance made me feel like I could do anything," the note stated. "Thank you for showing the world that we don't need to see to dream big."

Another came from a single mother in Canada, whose kid had been born with a mobility handicap. "You've given my son someone to look up to," she wrote. "Every time you took to the dance floor, it felt like you were dancing for him."

These notes were a continuous reminder to Chris that his path wasn't only his own. It belonged to the numerous others who recognised themselves in his narrative, who found hope and bravery in his steps. It was a shared victory, one that stretched well beyond the Glitterball Trophy.

## THE CONTINUING LEGACY

In the months and years that followed, Chris's life transformed in ways he hadn't imagined. The experiences on Strictly had not only impacted his profession but also his sense of purpose. While humour remained his passion, his platform had increased, allowing him to push for more inclusiveness and representation in ways that felt very personal.

He collaborated with groups focussing on accessibility in the arts, utilising his narrative to underscore the need of breaking down barriers for artists of all abilities. He became a voice for individuals who had been neglected, speaking at conferences and meetings on the need for diversity—not just as a concept but as a reality.

Yet, Chris was always ready to shift the spotlight away from himself. When questioned about his effect, he typically answered, "I didn't do this alone. This was a team effort—Dianne, my family, everyone who supported me. And every person who observed my trip thought, 'Maybe I can accomplish that too.' That's where the actual effect is."

**A MESSAGE THAT ENDURES**
Chris's path served as a reminder that hope isn't something we find—it's something we build, step by step. His time on Strictly Come Dancing was packed with hardships, but it was also filled with discovery: of strength, of connection, and of what it means to embrace life fully, especially when the route ahead appears unknown.

For the people who watched, who applauded, who felt their own boundaries begin to crumble as they saw Chris dance, the message was plain. Resilience isn't about being fearless—it's about going ahead in spite of the fear. It's about choosing to trust, to develop, and to show up, even when the chances seem stacked against you.

## CLOSING REFLECTIONS

As Chris exited the studio for the last time, his hand resting softly on Dianne's shoulder, he couldn't help but grin. He didn't need to see the empty stage behind him to know what it signified. It wasn't just the location where he'd learned to dance—it was the place where he'd learned to believe in himself in a manner he never had before.

For Chris, the adventure didn't finish with the Glitterball Trophy. It was simply the beginning of something far greater—a legacy of optimism, tenacity, and the unwavering idea that when we push above our boundaries, we can alter not just our own lives but the lives of everyone watching.

Printed in Great Britain
by Amazon